A Birthday Wish

Wonderful Surprises

By Flavia and Lisa Weedn
Illustrated by Flavia Weedn

Cedco Publishing · San Rafael, California

ISBN 0-7683-2153-0

Text by Flavia and Lisa Weedn
Illustrations by Flavia Weedn
© Weedn Family Trust
www.flavia.com
All rights reserved.

Published in 2000 by Cedco Publishing Company.
100 Pelican Way, San Rafael, California 94901
For a free catalog of other Cedco® products, please write to the
address above, or visit our website: www.cedco.com

Printed in Hong Kong

1 3 5 7 9 10 8 6 4 2

Book and jacket layout by Teena Gores

The artwork for each picture is
digitally mastered using acrylic on canvas.

Life is a miracle,

and birthdays are

gifts.

Each

year

comes

wrapped

in a

ribbon

of dreams . . .

and

whether

you

are very *young*.

or very *old*,

or

somewhere

in

between,

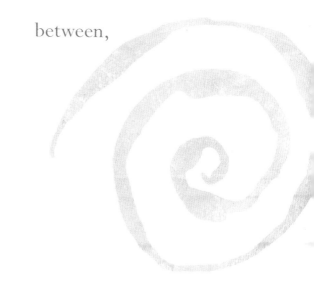

life is

filled with

wonderful

surprises.

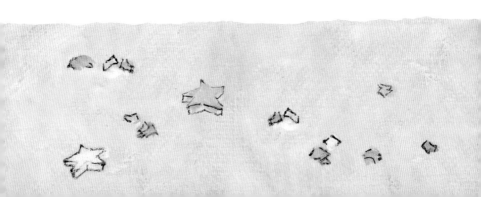

So,

when

you stand

beside

your

may you

hear

the *wish*

I make,

a wish

that your

birthday

wish

comes *true.*